Yo-Yo Ma

World Musician

by Lou Ann Walker

CELEBRATION PRESS
Pearson Learning Group

Contents

A Cello Superstar

Yo-Yo Ma is a famous **cellist**, but he is not like most cellists. He loves to play rock and jazz music, as well as **classical** music. He even played music for an action movie.

Many people think that Yo-Yo Ma is a cello (CHEL loh) superstar. He has sold millions of **albums**. He has also won many music awards, including Artist of the Year.

This **superb** musician was only five years old when he gave his first public concert. When he was seven he played on television. Since then he has performed for people around the world. He has appeared on television on *Sesame Street*® and in famous concert halls like Carnegie Hall in New York City.

Cellist Yo-Yo Ma stands with violinist Itzhak Perlman at the 2001 Academy Awards®.

In this book you will learn that Ma is more than just a **performer**. He wants to help audiences understand classical music. He enjoys introducing music by new **composers**. He is also interested in how **cultures** connect through music.

The Child Genius

Yo-Yo Ma has always been a part of more than one culture. He was born in Paris, France, on October 7, 1955. His parents were from China.

As a child, Yo-Yo Ma lived in a Paris neighborhood like this one.

Ma's mother and father chose a Chinese name with a special meaning for their son. "Yo-Yo" means "friend." True to his name, Ma has always made friends through music.

When Ma was young, his family did not have much money. They still found a way to keep music in their lives. Ma's father was a music teacher. He **analyzed** music **technique**. His mother was an opera singer. She thought of music as something people felt with their hearts.

At first Ma played the violin as his older sister did. However, he did not think he was a good violin player. Then he saw a double bass (bayss) and wanted to play this giant instrument. He was only four years old and too little for something so big. His parents suggested the cello.

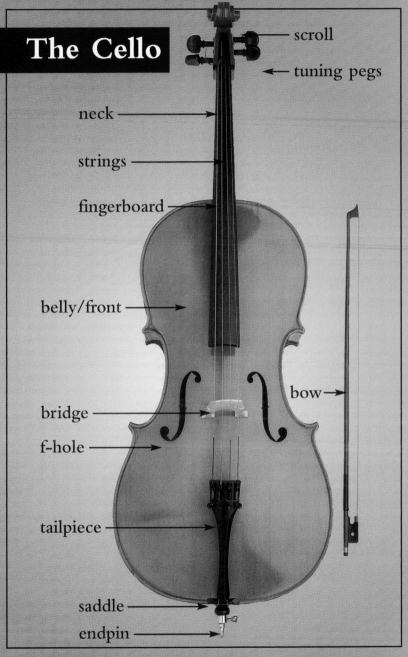

The Cello

scroll

tuning pegs

neck

strings

fingerboard

belly/front

bow

bridge

f-hole

tailpiece

saddle

endpin

This music page is an example of the kind of cello music Yo-Yo Ma learned.

No one could find a cello small enough for Ma. So his father created one. He put a long metal endpin on the end of a cello. That put the cello higher. Ma sat on a pile of three telephone books to pull the bow across the strings.

Each day Ma's father gave him two measures or sections of difficult music to memorize. "I used to practice only five to ten minutes a day," Ma said. For those few minutes he worked hard. He made each part perfect before he moved on to the next. He clearly was a musical **genius**.

The Rebel Years

When Yo-Yo Ma was only five, the famous musician, Isaac Stern, heard him play. He knew Ma was special. Stern wanted Ma to have the best teachers. So in 1962 the family moved to New York City.

Moving to America meant learning about a new culture. At first Ma was shy. He would only whisper to his teachers. Yet in school, where he spoke English, he was expected to speak up. At home Ma's family spoke only Chinese.

Ma had trouble dealing with these two worlds. When he began studying at a well-known music school, he began to skip classes. He wanted to get away from the many rules at school and at home.

When Ma was 12 he went to the Professional Children's School. There his teachers put him in harder classes to keep him from getting bored. He did well and graduated from high school at the young age of 15.

The summer after high school, Ma went to music camp. It was his first time away from home. Suddenly he felt free.

"I went wild," Ma said. He didn't go to practice. He even left his cello out in the rain. However, his new freedom helped Ma become more creative.

After camp, Ma went to Columbia University. College felt too much like high school because he still lived at home. Isaac Stern thought that Ma might like Harvard University near Boston better. He was right.

While at Harvard Ma gave so many concerts he did not have enough time for his schoolwork. So, his father told him to slow down and perform only one concert a month. "I'm happy I followed his advice," Ma said.

Isaac Stern (left) performs with Yo-Yo Ma (right) at Carnegie Hall in 1991.

The Traveling Musician

In 1978 Ma began to play with major orchestras. He traveled as the first single winner of the Avery Fisher Prize, an award for outstanding work in music.

A young Yo-Yo Ma performed many concerts after winning the Avery Fisher Prize.

Yo-Yo Ma rehearses before a concert.

Ma also recorded music by his favorite composers. These were Franz Joseph Haydn and Wolfgang Amadeus Mozart. One music expert said that when Ma played Haydn's fast music notes, it sounded like the cello had "burst into chuckles."

Yo-Yo Ma plays music by Bach on a television program called "The Music Garden."

Ma's greatest joy as a musician has been playing a concert of all Johann Sebastian Bach music. "For an entire evening, I'm living in a great man's mind," Ma said.

Ma has two beautiful and very old cellos. He loves one of them so much, he calls it "sweetie pie." When Ma travels by airplane, the cello he takes gets its own seat on the plane.

Yo-Yo Ma is shown with his cello after a rehearsal at Carnegie Hall.

New York police officers returned Yo-Yo Ma's cello after he left it in a taxi.

However, accidents can happen. Once Ma forgot a cello in the trunk of a taxi. The cello was worth $2.5 million. The taxi driver turned the cello in to the police. Ma was very happy when he got the cello back. "The cello is my voice," he said.

The Teacher

Even though Yo-Yo Ma has a busy concert schedule, he always finds time for young musicians. He often teaches master classes in the cities where he performs.

Yo-Yo Ma listens to Tseng Yu-Ting as she plays during a master class.

A master class is taught to gifted students by an expert such as violinist Isaac Stern. Students are eager to learn from Yo-Yo Ma because he is the best cellist in the world. Ma enjoys working with young people because they are so excited about music.

Isaac Stern teaches students at a music workshop in 1995.

After presenting a master class, Yo-Yo Ma signs autographs for students and fans.

When Ma works closely with students, he may borrow their instruments to show them something. Then he will listen to them play. If they talk about being tired, he tells them to look for energy from the rest of the orchestra.

New Challenges

Yo-Yo Ma is always looking for new ways to play cello music. He has played country-style and folk music with other musicians. He also records children's music.

Yo-Yo Ma played "Appalachian Waltz" with cellist Edgar Myer (left) and fiddler Mark O'Conner (right).

A Main Route of the Silk Road

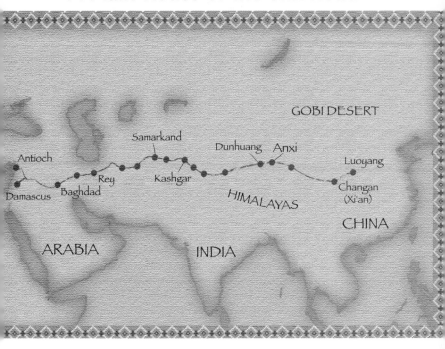

To stretch himself further, Ma began his Silk Road Project in 1998. Long ago, **merchants** traded from China, through Central Asia, then to India, and across Iran. The project brings together musicians from these lands.

Yo-Yo Ma (left) performs with Silk Road musicians
Kayhan Kalhor (center) and Siamak Jahangiri (right).

Through the Silk Road Project, Ma has
planned many festivals. His goal is to
introduce people from around the world
to different cultures. Ma said, "Music
can act as a magnet to draw people
together."

Ma continues to face challenges. One is finding enough time for his family. It helps that his wife, Jill, and their children, Nicholas and Emily, are all musicians. So most of the time he can bring the world of music together with his family.

Yo-Yo Ma with his wife, Jill Horner

Glossary

albums   recordings of music or speech on records, tapes, or CDs

analyzed   examined carefully

cellist   person who plays the cello

classical   more formal types of music

composers   people who write music

cultures   the beliefs and traditions of a group of people

genius   someone extremely smart or talented

merchants   people who buy and sell goods

performer   someone who performs, or presents something onstage

superb   splendid

technique   the way physical movements are used in playing a musical instrument